Nedobeck's Numbers Book

by

Don Nedobeck

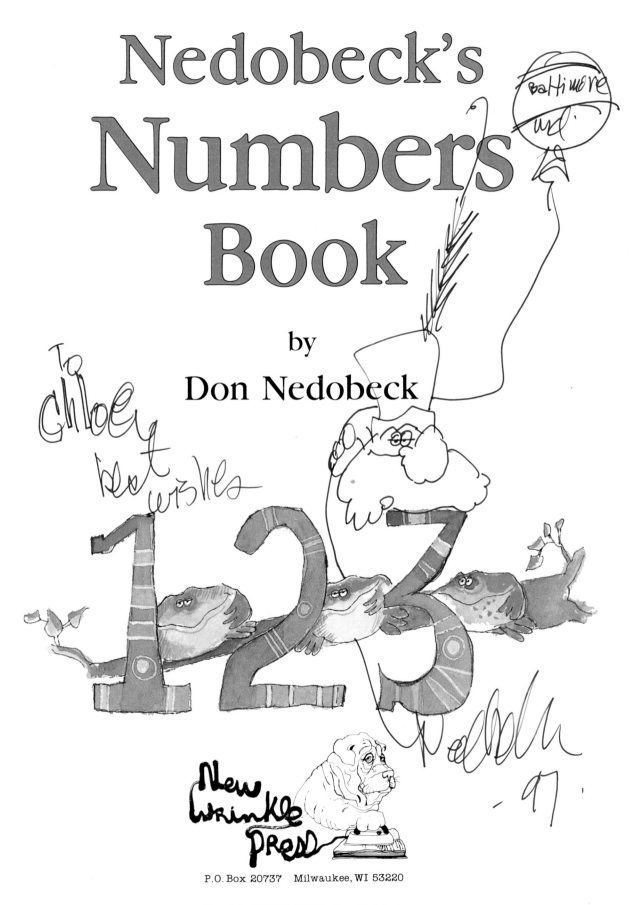

New Wrinkle Press

P.O. Box 20737   Milwaukee, WI 53220

ISBN 0-944314-01-5

Let's learn the numbers **one** through **ten**.

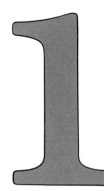

One shaggy sheep dog

2 Two colorful cats

3 **Three** three-toed
tree toads

sitting in a tree

 **Four** fancy fiddlers

fiddling   what they fancy

5 **Five** flying fish

flying freely

6 Six
wise
owls

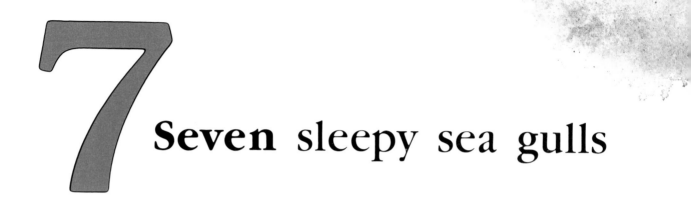

7 Seven sleepy sea gulls

standing in the sand

8 **Eight**

great bears
on tiny
wooden
chairs

Nine happy hippos

10

Ten
tall
giraffes

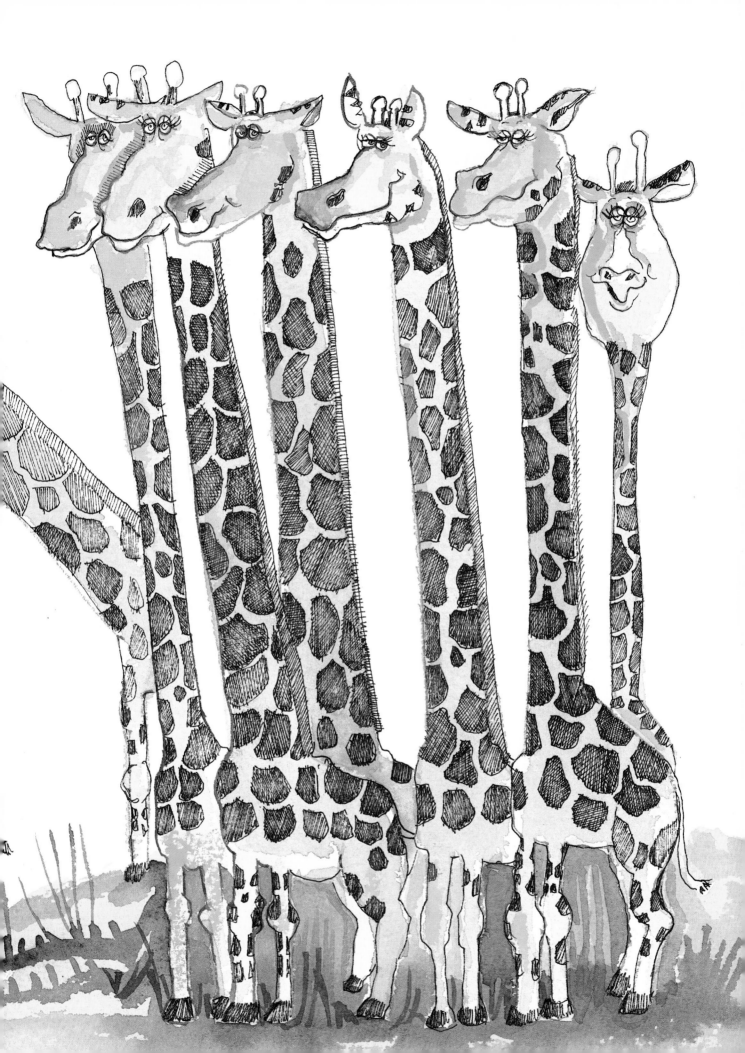

3 **Three** pigs and

2 **two** ducks

you can't forget

make up the **five** **5** animals

in the Barnyard **Quintet!**

Molly knows and feels quite smug
that **four quarts** fill

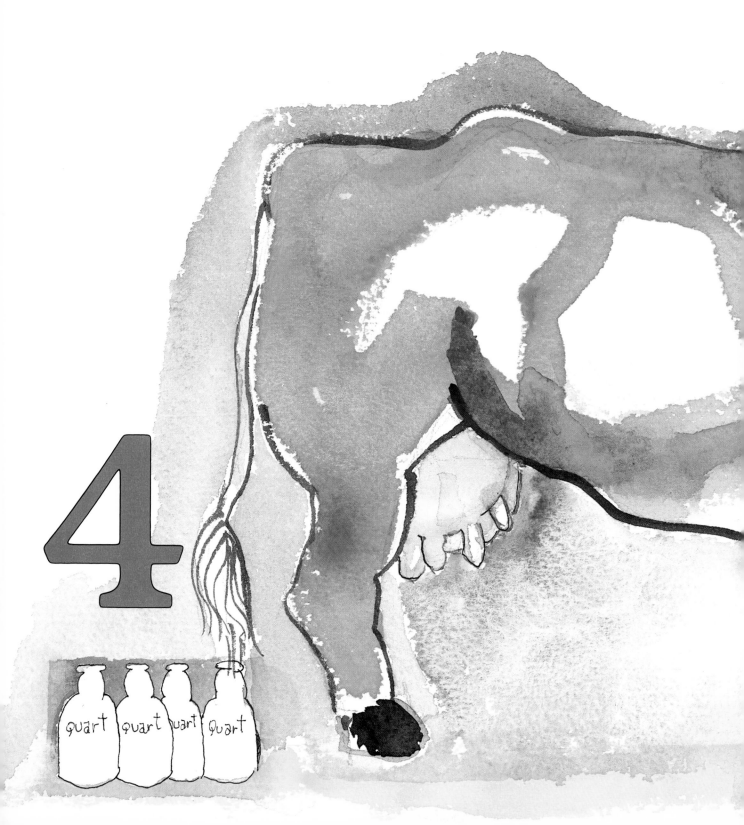

a **one gallon** jug.

Harriet and Hazel Hen

lay **12**

twelve eggs
inside their pen—
an even **dozen!**

One through **ten,**
aren't numbers fun?
Now let's go back
to number **one!**